MW00749465

THE MOOD
EMBOSSER

THE MOOD EMBOSSER

LOUIS CABRI

COACH HOUSE BOOKS

first edition

Published with the assistance of the Canada Council for the Arts
and the Ontario Arts Council

The Canada Council Le Conseil des Arts
for the Arts du Canada

ONTARIO ARTS COUNCIL
CONSEIL DES ARTS DE L'ONTARIO

NATIONAL LIBRARY OF CANADA
CATALOGUING IN PUBLICATION DATA

Cabri, Louis
    The mood embosser

Poems.
ISBN 1-55245-095-3

    I. Title.

PS8555.A2415M66 2001   C811'.6   C2001-904045-8
PR9199.4.C22M66 2001

*A book
for Nicole Markotić*

Poetry is information.
– L. Zukofsky

The Mood Embosser

0   The Importants of Being 12
Fey lure 24
The Good Beaver (1996) 30

1   'truth build up' 36
'social logic' 37
'unconscious needs' 38
'accident accumulates intent' 39
Disposed 40
'Guatemala ... ' 45

0   Grind on 48
Slung low – *sell high* 51
Clone jacking 53
Curdles 55

1   Posy 78
Yield 79
perma 80
So how's the Dow 81
Grease Earn 85

0   Cornius Flakius, 92
WELCOME TO THE GAS AGE 102
And Sean Connery 107

1   A remumblery 110
I project 123
Alan Davies Project 127

0   138 138

0

The Importants of Being

In economics
negligible.

      My
           action

                Cheerios
                   still-life
                      went
                            soggy!

Adopt
a dollar.

Good investors
fight human nature at every turn.
 — *Verbatim* letter to fund

holders. Words

only

combine many in
so ways. Built-in
self-critique

'naturally'
"unheeded"

"'"
.

      My
           kindling

---

                              memories
                                   of
                                        impressionistic
                                             paintings!

Pain
management program
in the real world,
a heel's hurl,
the eel world.

Social
travesty
relations.

          My
                    need

_____

                    for
                              more
                                        social
                                             unformation!

Punctuation management program.

'Male penetration
doubts. No one
to talk to.'

to gawk at
your *own mind*
bores ... how
interesting for 'you'
must be
where exactly?

To the penetralium!

    My

        I

_____

                an

                      article

                            of

                                  fright!

Dull straight way asks
next perfectly flat direction.

Who won – The World or North America?

It's been ice
proving
talking with you
beneath it. Instructions
came from
bank.

Like borrowing
presidential veto
pen for Home Ec.
class.

    My

        rumball

_____

                digested

                    and

                          in

                            circulation!

To the UN Charter of Human Rights!

The charge of the credit card.

Transaction complete
when money
'ejaculates' between
hands.

Glands of a devolutional, enterprising squirt
maker.

Whale-Nazi, govern by microbe
the social plankton
masses

      My

           bio

---

                  banging
                      cargo
                            case
                                  load!

in your
state
tub

it's germ
welfare

out here

      My

           couldn't

---

                                    agree
                                        with
                                            your
                                                more!

gerrymandering
the gene pool.

Tonsil eyes.
Terrible pace.

Snoring gills.

Swaying pate
angling crowd for votes.

The petting meaning.

        My
                frivolously
_____

                        twirl
                            at
                                tether's
                                    end!

Ironic fowl,

fool,

fill.

'Are there new emotions in the kitty.'

I'd love you, too, in Carrara

marble. Monitor 3.
Tear duct in cheap seats

pearled. Camera 5.

Uninhabited stadium

of social being. Uninhabited heart of the

social being.

Being social
choke.

Being rout
about
something.

Body root sound
root!
Rout for
being just
about
root.
Echo rout.
Boxing shouts, being shorts.

Crude-oiled Jonathan-Seagull.
Bituminized Jiffy Pop expressivity.
Sedimental you.

Clay-borne ventriloquism.

Shots.

Nervous about historical convergences
social repertoire shrank
– which *they* didn't mind in the least –
including spending – which they
did.

Under guise of
trodden on and thrown aside
willingly Nerfed
to 'air' resistance.

      My

          late

               October

                   for

                       what?

                           fest!

Spongiform-worthy whiteness
on the dotted line
interpolating horizon

flow.

Run over.

The social body
burbed

– on civics.

Bears body.

Secluding habits.

Winterizing polemicism.

Playing dusk.

Our mind, our
shed. Instruments
came from
bank.

Subsequently Leigh went into finance.

Poetry's Law of Diminishing Marginal Utility.

Reversed, next
metre reading.

Petro-Canada Poet Laureates of the Peter
Gzowski Invitational Golf Tournament.

'What a responsible person to write about.'

Their turmoil, our terms.
Our 'their', their *ow*.
Symmetry that knowledge brings

      them theme.

          To a balloon, laden with knowledge

          one head at a time. (*'Sharks for Beginners.'*)

              Knowledge contained in

          Tiny bubble darts over hairline, eyes

    a mythical concept, confused,

        fixed on glory.

of yielding, shapeless associations.

In the corridors of hours,
out of halls,
into malls

My
love

Emma
Goldman's
political
hair!
out of malls,
into halls

On launching some bottles
With knowledge mind-borne

Creational boondoggle or museum
Of mad appurtenances the Coca

Cola Museum I do not know
What could have entitled you

To the surname of 'the mad man'
For I am sure you are consistent enough

Inveighing with bitterness
Against yourself and all others

Except Mother, Father
Fiancée, Boss

And Friend
Who

stoked your
stork?

Anyway, *our
oil.*

Ghost denoters for.

Psychology to spy for.

Pay.

Doin' it, but for emendations
our way. Peter picked
paper on literacy.

Sashay   can you see

Fame's dancefill.

What you're made of?

– Whose bottle are you on, in,

after?
Round of heaves
on the house.

'Tosspots and brooding loners'
need apply

it. 'O world's wasted wax!'

     My
         the

                    unword
                         unbeing
                              of
                                   disprepossession!

Mama was a running pie.

Legislation and sausages.

Bumper stickers, windows. Mirrors,
haircut.

Get a new coin

operated discussion
going – fifty cents to
correct answer none
volunteered
immediately. Nervous
yet machine-liked.
Cookies *into* the slot.
Graphics pie chat.

            Percy change

            Or prop up or pot
            down the sensitive
            plant of good weed-

            ing in these wangled, tangl-
            ing bins of scrib-
            bliture, renderingly

            unworked –
            Change chance
            operations on

your life with this
edible plant.

Working out
kinks of meaning
flex.
Burn

off, at every turn, on

JERK II

My
action
kindling
need
I
rumball

bio
couldn't
frivolously
late
love
the.

Beansprouts and clouts.

*I was a contract
of Worship
underwritten by
Life Force One*

Fey lure

When links and levers leave us after a
Societal deboning pounding
   Hamilton Against Poverty
Enter 'the level playing field'
   Grave, 'tits up'
In toxins game
   Party favours crooked
Backs the lacking
   Scruple offs
The name gain – legacy of socialism
   Only if that's the definition you use
For poverty – 'does it exist', enthalpy of
   Vocabulary where *e*, capacity for work
Equals chord o' code
   Marked 1 or 0 in
Regulation time
   Ditto remakes
Remarks a longhand
   Squall for last cast
Male dressed member only
   Affordable protein – please demonstrate
To the election-erect: *Wear a condom*
   Mulroney's born every minute I
Can make a difference need
   Million-dollar vacation too
Plastered to gauze the hospital press
   On to Ottawa 15th May
To pan for bedding
   Care, not cuts
Info bytes my back
   Pay *hurt* masking defeat tape
The Grateful Dead type reward
   Reword 'Raise your dead

To the pay [-off], malted Canadian ... '
  That's burial pits gravel
Against peaches
  Square D Canada Electric Port
Colbourne Job Loss 161
  To procedures which I am
Textual processes of
  Texan sex parchment
A strip-named object
  Sung or kicked
Distances this
  Discontinuous arrival
L'arriviste
  SquareD against harsh temperaments but
Trapped by same
  Death body obsession
With integrative possession passes
  Whole through hole of subject
Position at intersection
  Of a synchrony (*cf.* sensory system of average office tower)
With internal law ('boom learning to sprawl ... ')
  Of memory receptual
Imprints lines of
  Representation over over decades of peace, friendship and alliance
From narrative machinery
  Needs follow – beware (the
Rolfing motor goes, Snickers snack ...)
  Stunting by indifference
Slopes of inference
  From feelings (Dear Grief Spasm)
Structural bust – *get a* shelf *life*
  Unbearable Lightness Of
Self first
  Cause 'cause
It's Slinky maverick

Goner nucleates into speech
'I'm afre*u*d of talk!'
'MAKE MY EFFECT'
'Unwind from this, yoyo' (– public spooling
For loose threads
Tailored advantage coated
Hangers
On to go …)
'By the way, I walk
I'm a man – no, time to talk … '
'Sentimental Coward!'
Self-actuating sweat-on piping mother
Tongue condition – literally
Writing on the past – the work producing pad
And pen, evidence   ‑
Before it's lost the most
Normalizing inequities experience
Recession from sensual liminal exteriors
Into conscious
A discretely *must self* perpendicular
To the grind like an axiom
Charged
Electrofusive plaint hardly
Stroked – prepaid *all* the way
Would you prefer it
Proven right for the wrong reasons or
Situationiste d'abord absorbed
Knowledge of the G-spots
In social space celebrate dish of 500
Frontier channels
Brain cycle
Figurehead briefly unpopular returns packing
'One helluva lunch
Spaghetto
If only you'd'a swung from the *tees*'
The people's *pig*

Nasty piece o' nasty
Door-to-door stain remover – *compare value*
Unsleeving pump action
Idiot proof drunk
Too much a wealth debt
To be serious these
Temperate slopes harvest moon glimmers
Quaint – insecticidal
Sheen by day hic prostate waits for you outside
The untoward union united
States 'our' power
Missed wrist shot off
Pluriversal franchise
After Oct 26 no-confidence vote
Wasted, was already dead
Opportunity to debate beside the point
Being undebated
Condition which can't be machine-tooled
Fundamentally eVades for Representation
He is a junior apparel manufacturer
She is evicted from building
You want an unconscious, for guidance
Over grid, *frisson*, swingin' ataraxy
Power want
Sculpts reason's cake we're filled by
Verdiction, delimiting self as a ga-
By south-polar mood
Rubbed hearings roll form
Nouns of action deposits
In cells
-Teria models the
Cakewalkout being
Known being one tell whose I across
The surface tact
Body we're
Part of

Offer to
'Accept all you can … '
From Sea to Shining Can
Bank on the unbanked
Float on …
Liberty Island Committee of the Provisional Government 1837
'Yes, Kim, I'm one of the enemy'
I Went Crazy With KISS
A GM Transmission to destroy
Windsor 700 Jobs
Died P & H Foods 130 Jobs
1992 Champion Sparkplugged 180
Jobs Control Systems
1984–Present
For Rob Manery, MA Canadian
Tire 'more than a tire … '
Storegeneration
X loves
Y Z at end variable
Aspersion units *assault*
The gearbox drives
Don'ts revive, drink and
Stiffen him for two
Lovers find the penis
Much like a third party
NDP emphatic and in
1991 in the fore
Skin a bauble
Droops – thus, conserve your options
On perspective, prospectus male response
Easily quarters slots
Machine consumer
Resistance movement in your
Chrome man anon
Anon I must
Keep movin' on

Can't stand still
Ford Canada's mobile
   Capital signs
Closed shave
   To reflection: *Consider your captions*

The Good Beaver (1996)

'What is to be feared more than death?'

I remember well the Chelsea
rack and pinion agency
cross-country chuck-up
checkered flags
tabula gaza that John locked onto for

nestled in the café, vacuum-sealed
fresh from but this voice
   yes, this voice –

    I am bulgar, hear my
    refrigerator 'girlish' temper
    verbal icebox
    in the silty light, Muppets on ice

You've cracked
my bucket,
your stomping on

petunias
This spud's fore
plotted

A gear is born
with you in mind – not
against you, *with* u
haul T-bone
heart-staked

for hear the service chime
for read the safety card
then scupper your willies
for accent the sloping
seniority of erections
for a manifesto
is born independent
representative
slow
pan
surd on the run in
the partying stocking
shot – too many
jurassic checkpoints induced
industrialization by foreign capital bumpy
on the fingers when money
feels normal on the road
'again' to the strawberry social
body dangerously close to
historical consciousness – reclassified:
Ford pickup ad's transcending lyric

> *I remember well*
> *the song 'Zip to my dong'*
> *for givens forgive not*
> *thy 'thee', Quimquim*

is a taloned context
ideology temperate
loading zone, page or disk sector – a chip off
blocked agency
'multinational problem' bone in
caption reads *Ray* – instead of *Ron* – *Charles*
reporting for CBC TV

Syntax, all hail.

'Owing to inclement weather, the social revolution occurred in poetry'

– resonances
resin
or residence (travel-section readers, take note)
in our ears?

Sorry, wrong private sphere.

'Recolonize the signifier!'
Movement in self blossoming
swill, a turd elect
are off their bowls
(need word 'heliotrope' in here, shit
for brains let the Muzak in
hand, the man
Gail Lee:
'I speak as spaghetti to you, meatball,
Of plate tectonics and geography,
Cruise missiles in '83, and prairie
Silos 'stroyed in '95!'
Oh take me back
alive, with the band, in hand
of the man, Gail Lee!

In this scenario it is
nothing
it is nothing
while the economy declines, morale

disintegrates, investment evaporates, society
polarizes

experiencing
victory in your life
ringside.

Advance to harm level.

June frog, July bug,
August retrospective. Light to call your own
moth. Death watch, bosun's tweet,
afterdinner cigar.

'I was taxed to behave.

"That" way

lies the body shop
unctuating performatives

Did you say *Pass me the ketchup* – or – *Pass me, or catch up, but don't* something

"Disillusion."

Up here we beat ourselves every morning with a stout stick of maple, crying out ritual apologies in a Show Trial for the Fabian betterment of humankind – well before taking our cuppa, stretching the cat, sorting and neatening closets and cupboards, and sitting down for a half-hour in a stiff-backed chair with a brisk dramatic poem in iambic tetrameter and rhyming couplets and characters with faintly exoticized dialects. Then, we get on with what we call the day's business – whittling sticks.

Yours, Earle

1

truth build up

borders

exorcised by commemorative plaques

social logic

gets lethargic and semantic

fields

like favours

like

unconscious needs

conscious subject   runs

over itself to

encircled forms to

subject a habitation

grim minder with gaps

speech economics plunder

'petrol costs

less than bottled water'

accident accumulates intent

intention action

consequence more important than goal

Disposed

For want
    Ad
on yas tsuJ
    rorriM
Yes to luge's roarin'
    Arraign your horses, consider
Your cat
    Under the lash, the eye
That smoke gets in
    Your falsies 'teased
To plead "you'"
    Name the pun
Amends
    2D talks interactive
Pointer-stick body
    To be, or want
That is, investment
    Crust to crest, jest
The beefy I (crèched

On credit …) deal in surfaces
And intercourse seams
Less safe out
Skirts fashion faceplate
Display April '94
Frill for more
Dupe loops **Deadly**
Grunt tubes – Caution
Punch line
Exposed! Nude from Dordogne
To Provence Snowboard Women Who Rule
A Girl's Own Lexicon
We Love: Our Thirst
Annual Rebuke
'Progressive' Game Anglers
Pick Your Piste, Make Your Mogul
Holiday '93 $2.95
Goal of the catalogued
Goal, folds and
Goals of folds captious
Love-lexis by
Sortilege, enemy's
Lack speech
Impedance tropes
Refused to fight
'Good balking to you'
Bateman nature
Cartoonist meets glob-
Al organon, scoping
Tropes sale
Of vessels doped to cauterize
Transcendent head
Chafed at
Historical bit
Part I am clouded in
Others have paid for (*live*

Feed now)
Griff vertigo where
   No referent hasbeen gone before
Ego chaos machine
   Eat or die! logical
Interlude from the reper
   Tory lubes 'the bod public'
Was now corpsed
   Bornag
Raph*aeli*c desires are there
   Behind the penis (The Puck Stops Here!)
Two credible witnesses?
   Or's Latin tame matin robs worm
Biggest threat to self's labellous
   Governing turn ˉ
A tune a
   Tuna deep
Melt instead
   If given own organs, will
Mired (True
   Fucked-Off and Amazed Stories
'Why me? Why now? Why
  . My brain is in the way?'
Purged to bucket
   Trends) 'Mine'
In park
   In out
Your head in knocks
   Ternal command super
Stitches nest
   Self patching on/off
MR-READE
   On 'e' but
You really need 'r'
   In thee find the
Cost of talent

Your best, not your waste
Ode to Perishable Good
   Work kills per
Signature
   Legislation signifying
Our interests in name only, *vamp*
   While managing their own
Pet sibylline clamours
   Finally gets their own
Back dated
   Golf Kings
Swing Jamaica
   Noticeable career path?
Directory of over 2,300 dog breeders
   Industrial city
3,000 x Flin Flon, 3 x Dallas, closer than Taiwan
   You'll tide future world-class production sharing Mexico
'Take the lexicon to Mexico'
   Competition's con petition
Company 'I Wanna be
   Erected' how
To coping saw
   Mirror-marks
False society
   Breeding to the inverted
Comportment
   Alized plutocracy
Of back-formations
   Lacks formed
Looney Tune utopia
   Vol. 17. No. 1 Florida Showcase
Exculpated outcomes
   Chosen, odds for outcomes chosen, wager
      amount and potential payout
Organized on a corporate basis and has a juridical
   personality, governed by present statutes,

regulations approved by its organs and articles of the civil
   'Life' a biological fluid, is not entirely safe
Dear body without a licence
   Addressed in exoteric language
At the UNPROFOR reception centre
   What's the glossy damage on you?
We want to come away from this
   Feeling empowered, surrender
Your token only a
   Somatic frag
Divided, labours
   Spoken for
NAUSEA announces: 'We have iterability'

Guatemala, El Salvador, Cuba, Mexico, Angola, Mozambique:
'We can't deficit-spend the world into prosperity anymore.'

Drug-resistant malaria, flesh-eating bacteria, viruses like Ebola, AIDS:
Give me a documented outbreak and a reported profit that follows

us? This is Winnipeg. I've never cried in my life.
Face

to face
this? Capitalist

neologians, necrophiliac
devotions: commitment, integrity, results –

that's my B&S practice.
Concord of terms hustle

buts out door,
make a dash of it –

Angostura bitters.
All souled out,

sociodegradable identities
in. 'I owe it to you.'

Which doctors
the facts

elsewhere. After
use, fold

away
toward

another meat eater
in square dwelling.

0

Grind on

Well-insulated
with Gore-Tex
from fog
and drizzle

and with context
from
an arch fiend – The
Mood Embosser.

Self
raised
dot of braille. Father finger
sensitive.

.

Dryness in the apartment?
Feeling blank – like paper?
Stanzaic room, sitting stance?
Activity whose

environment organizes specific rules and conventions
determining status, nature, structure,
use. Gazoo through
Flintstones'

TV
contacts
boss:
'Can I go now?'

.

It's part
cortex
governing heart
muscles now proven susceptible

to stress were it not for
'the beak of ego', laser-tool
polisher and resurfacer
of semiotic rubble.

Yes, peck.
No. (peck)
Yes.
Na.

.

Nature programs convey seniority of ecosystems
we don't understand and are destroying
at rates on par with every disease's mutational
reappearance in young bodies.

Owen against a horse
and fifty years later Surin
against the Formula 1: What is context?
2. What is poetry, anyway?

Count to fifty, subtract
age, multiply what
you have to muster an
answer like no other

prancing misnomer
is handsomer while algorhythms
of Al Gore
grind on.

.

Their low
blows to soft
tips butterfly
onto toothpick

in stentorian light
at a Game Boy picnic
'Let the lows blow.'
Flush feint

to left margarine
on 'corn kernel'
to write
'Keep the Colonel frying.'

.

Moves furnished and with vestments
of expertise
for later sedentary expression
brings in missing the mission itself

to present indicatively
a mandate
for imperatives
licenced to behave as if normal

in the arena of sound
as judgement upon X
set this
tale.

Slung low – *sell high*

Giving up the light before it's turned on.
Corruptive agency.

Room pitch to screen.
To get the entirely expected out of each one.

They move the figures onto their ground.
'New hope for the found.'

Shadows steam.
Features clocked to rhyme.

Home rubs corners with it.
Just another phase for 'Glad to get this time'.

To get it, this time.
Lips assertion, swollen.

Days of cuts.
Has to be going on all the time.

Where stabilized does it reach.
Couldn't harrow marrow fast enough to bear it.

'Not' in throat.
Perceptibly expanding.

Not/Always here.
Ever going to leave.

Retreats.
Say, did you happen to – Say something.

Newspapers read/unread.
Today is the greatest – Day of the pie.

Imagination verses.
Great halls o' knowledge.

Bringing up for questioning.
To suck the big one small and the small one big.

'Cannibal?'
'You can!'

Clone jacking

three for two
in the rut

of *New!* a
day on the

chin keep your
head on screen

saver it
waiting to

happen the
surface con

ducked er went
on strike pun

drippings coat
tongues coat hang

ur suspense
suspender

spender his
'n' hers furs

down in a
fur ball up

in fire all
X pensive

pens sieve cheer
cheese fang club

the dollar
club the seal

scout the perm
it cinched belt

drive out loud
guns la morhde!

la morhde! la
– *du yu havf*

aay leessauwns
forrh zatt mess

age? blank-blank!
'WE HAVE DOO

DLE PARI
TY' 'partly!'

**Bored Red Left
for Right Bored**

**Red Left for
Right Bored Red**

Left for Right
'three for two'

Curdles

The Brain is 80% rain,
cold, verging on
refusal – 'It won't start'. And yet, and yet
the Bourgeois Brain is our joie
moves to inner laws consistently
   desiring gem status, on stem,
   in a museum of muses it
     has befuddled.

… This is its story.

  be my
  hokey poetry

  look at the words
  look at the birds outside

  the lyrical wonderland that is you
  begs for spirit in a bone

  look at these stones try
  explaining why a fun-cake like you was left out in the rain

  in the dated way ads have of remixing
  'creative juices are a beautiful thing', look at you

All quietism feeds is a front

Don't think because the frame's useless
it doesn't apply.
                    (… needs
                        is a font?)
'Don't seam me in.'
Huh? We're used to the outer limits.
I once took a tram
to bourgeois consciousness
thunderlining in clouds
dispersing over city
dump. Move on, out of crystals,
to mighty exteriors, they told me at
the gates, police
of mind where it is usual to ask
What condones the association?
As in, What's for breakfast.
'Mind' the convenience of a sack
'Mind' the cog gap
'Mind' the metre checked monthly
'How are you today?'
Break first, questions later. 'Nippy out there!'
Moving crystals, block to block.

I'd call it Tennyson's Lager Queen
                Mum's the label.
We had purpled our
livers to, peopled our hearts'
sandwich-board hunger for
– *Ignore him. 'Walk on'*
my mind, permanency of view
establishes crown,
disperses crowd
'troublesome brew'.

Gather ye …
skirts the issue. They tore up track!
We fielded our surprise
equidistantly
maintaining classic perspective.
'From each,
the other' slogan
was better, for results
– more evidence.
The revolution
/ min met industry
standards will be Internetted etc.
I will pay my gratuities, my annuities, stock
my fluids, and stoke my hold.
Signed _____ _____.
– Papermanency View Inc. –
I hear *The Burger Joy Conch* right now
read their liner notes out loud.
I believe in the tradition of shame and humility
in view of the fæces, I am a pervert. Dated __/__/__.
Hence, ethics.

Hence, limits.

'We

know

the

cap

is

a

thinking

drawer

for

a

crap.'

So present, the inside,
he's absent,

so inside the present
he's *passé,*

so outside the past, his own won't
last,

so past, the outside,
he's present

as an absence so lasts
he's *au courant.*

To be contained
to be continued.

Sleuthing sylphs tilt silt for numbers
to bare their fare –

stare – on automatic
vision – of escalators

By neck, the break
by state, the gate
by sale, the hail
by blues, the ruse

4
Here, lies

5
Past-tense satisfaction

over tense

past.

1
To Have Represented So Little
Cared For So Much
To So Few

2
To Have Represented So Few
Cared For So Little
For So Much

3
To Have Cared For So Little
Represented So Much
To So Many

6
… the insecticide I've been using
for my ideological problematic?
I didn't anticipate the 'weeds' vs 'flowers' problematic …

7
His secret tape worm oozing
from National Archives
4,000 hours long ... 37th president ...
at this point, so what
recuperative B-movie
gimmick next?

8
'Welcome to the eddies', flat-tones basso
Schwarzenegger.
'Bring your *Prose Edda*. It's a long ride.'

9
'We' 'have' 'come' 'to' 'the' 'end' 'of' 'the'
'noodle'.
Infinite fractions, it seems
over my belt buckle –
you discover *genuine* jewellery,
'tasteful but glittery'.

0
The sixties now spill
into zeroes.

The clash

of cash.

From the ground up
because ground down

from the continually new viewpoint
'refined', even …

Manifester

Do the imperative
   Start off.
    Go bad.
thing.

Higher tones
   Refrigerated
    cinnamon!
thing-out.

Spoiling for an inside
   'Its
    wickerness'.
out.

Expression
   Waves
    crusting.
were a sealing.

'Seasons in the sun ... '

1/ Red erosion begins on
what was always
considered *invasion from Mars*
anyway – right ... ?

The grain
of gain falls
mainly
with the
plane, yet out
of sight.
'That's right.'

Out of planes,
plans;
banks, 'development'.

Calibrated expertise –
        from sample to example,
        via type.

Square

Not much depends on
rush for Home Depot
wheelbarrows carry
cash enough to buy
scratch for a chicken

'Structural Adjustment'

The price of peas

and

qeues – however it's spelled

'Vaal speaks to you; you do not speak to Vaal!'
Scriptwriters may have been thinking Baal – *nor do I*
remember the runic tree alphabet; yet from the island's
steaming greens, I hungered for a sign.
Of course, they might be spelling it Val, *'valley girl',*
insider's joke? at least common Hollywood name
(just the other week, 'Val and the team' went undercover
in a world of high fashion).
The party continued into evening
the odds 'Vaal' would speak.

2/ Bearing respectfully in order
of putting them on – them
over ('fonly!),
in taking them off …

Put one on

end of fork where

it counts, go ahead, live

with the tines, points

well, eaten, down to shining

'Phil Johnsons'

for the team – *present*

participle? – city end of

your Batcave mouth

– *hero.*

Or if you like, I can store your head in the freezer.

Bad as

Their remains
to be said, not strewn;
stated, not drawn:
above and below as, 285–9
animals as, 86
asparagus as,
bag as, 86
balloon as, 364
box as, 86
branch as, 319
brothers and sisters as, 358
burglar as, 395
children as, 357
clarinet as, 86
etc.
    Pay to waken
from surrealistic
detritus.
    The indexed
word,

        alogical place
        in a logical space

aspires too

a ruled awakening

                Far below

                this 'flight'

                there is

I'm in a hemp suit, Dartmou‍
Road airport district

to me suggests
da Vinci's

dream, by
Freud, is today's sublime

gay travel market, and
I'm on fire, holding a key,

feeling generically
surreal, TV

leg-room

ad voiceover
in water   concluding: *Panning for*

a bearded   *surrealist*
                 control, in a world out

baby sculls   *of gold*
                 prospects!
the gurgling lake

Deep within this
'drive'   and no longer speaks

there is   to us DINK
a magazine cover,

                  scrawled 'on
young black soldier sal-
uting flag,   forehead', I

I'm in   think, as the drive
a barbershop, and Roland
                  continues
Barthes will address *the*
aggluti-   even

nation ... not only   having parked the car!
colonial occupation in

Algeria, but my
style of

cut – '*These turns*' (frantically gestures)
'*too predictable!*'

Full-justified four-point legalese was really taxing
my fibres, limbered to their
limits – I was a tree, after all
easily snapped
and none would hear me if I did:
teeth as, 37
tools as, 356
urinal as, 210
vermin as, 357

Retire on the rat
you've been saving

the last rhetorical flourish
for when fatally

cashed in.
Rat

symbol
elegant

distress-free
lifestyle – *I must have*

… stepped on one.

'Good for you!'

3/ The bottom line
('if there only was
one … ') needs cream
too …

4/ Complacency rules.
A stringent *No Filling-in-the-Blanks
Allowed*. Heard of it
before ... ?

sex and wars and tax cuts –
dire straits election

Pastoral democracy – herd
of it. Hence, the gadfly, and pies.
The Prince and the doily papers.
'Five stomachs hath the Fifth Estate ... '

See Dick's sperm wriggling into Jane's egg.

CCM's playoffs TV ad (2000), *He scores!*

'You *are too* gonna have that baby *and* get married.'

'*When* has it been so real? Oh, you fake fuck, right on.'

Toughing it out

fluffing it up

I eat Smurfs.

Turkeys in *my* contrail

are smoked and sliced

Trad flave, coming through.

Backward glance.

Troughing it out.

Die now save yourself and all future expenses.

The stern feather of comedy

Sanka little further in Perestroika Pernod.

We'll miss your numbers at checkout.

'And God gave himself a planetectomy', it replied.

'Someone's going to that ambulance for sure!'

'*Nice* pressure … '

'On *top* of the ambulance – oh my!'

Rhyme World

USA Today
Here's vomit on it

To a bald politician (NY, NY)

It's, like, I don't care about
the air in your hairs
but, in your care, the air's
'in your hair.'

for Calvin Trillin

Down with pollution!

OUR HANDS FOR
WHAT WE UNDERSTAND
Placarded plea – from who

cares to not
us, so our
hands don't

stand for
what
exactly

Words
outworn

outwards
wild

stallions
in

cigarette
ads

to
city

folk
with

no
cowboy

lore:
scallions.

January 1, 2001

1

Posy

want

you   what

mean   does

this

Yield

Rough, Gruff and Grim
and tiny Rin
tip-toed in

'Caught and bought!' – grim
gruff Rin, roughly
toe-tapped out.

perma

speak in
turn in
'a system
of differences'

to you
is great
for sense
makes reason

to me
in systems
they last
by names

for a while
in differences
reporting them
with relish

and division
with multiplication
their sales
are ourselves

So how's the Dow

    I dunno, how's it
    with you

In the float-based market
  capitalization index
    Sprung a leak

Of a public sphere
    In your face

Where attention accrues
  share liquidity
    There's condensation

It's best to use
  clear distinct strokes
    On ideas

Of a little less than
  a second a piece
    That fuck

And abhor disconnected details
    That

Are accountable
    To partitions

For as participants we're key
  informers
    '   '

Though not all analysts attach
  importance to performance
    – My wad

As an indicator of future profit
  levels

For temps and cardstock holders
    It's a mausoleum!

An indexical structure of brand relief
    The same

Is the afforded mechanism
    of compensation   For four, please

Within dominant environments   Like me

While systematic thought
    under topics   Being

Keeps squalor out and freshness   Sexed

In subject variations

The index constituency receives   A bar mitzvah!

Barring war, riot and natural
    disaster   – A breakneck fate

Preferential rates   Skimmed off

Even as vital signs decrease   Aplomb

Recession-resistant pharmaceuticals
    add shine and control   Resumes

To a portfolio's
    asset composition   Résumé

Whose will only two decades ago   Thunder

Spoke within eight years
    of retirement   Like a charm

As the security and
    intelligence service   Lily pad

To its captive client base

After in-house counselling

                      Floats

With public report updates

                      In high or low pressure
                      zones of

That namby-pamby crypto-communist
   left-wing NDP anti-NAFTA alliance

And other databases stand by

                      Retiary biostats

This plot of dials

                          A tingling in
                          the fingers

The hoped-for licenced cop's
   incensed tactics of refusal

                      Figures pointing

Polished with grift

From direct correlations of state-
   sponsored violence and public activism   To switch theorists

A Calvinist strain from the Tower
   of Babel

                          – Feebs

Tripling redemption fees in white
   and auxiliary heathen markets

                      Flush

Committed or permitted alignments
   in advance

                        To lust

As advertised traits

                      Mixer 'on'

Hired for results of total return

                          Dusting the
                          bongo drums

Merge cartels

To manufacture incidental

To providential

Insurances against obligation

For the shoes et cetera

Or ahnbahrah de shwah of rules

A body

Out-fit by deontological choke-pears

Surmises in welfare rococo

Corporate memory's coping pins ado

To indebt every cognate object

For interest-bearing account

Of swingin' the consonantal
   emporium –

Glamour

At the K-Mart of inscribing

Your 'yes' vote

Test-tube baby

Protocol

Fobs it off

As stack repair

Wears

Gymnosoph

Chapter

The end of

'Fuck you'

Let's split this spleen

Or mount

Or count

A diptych

A motto daub

for the barscheit *index*

Grease Earn

Hovering over	Her over a
La Guardia	Soapy-handed caress
Finds his market	Or a bank
Excels	Line up for food
Trueblood	And souvenirs
Gift horse	Of the city dump
Sells	Policy which repeats it
Responsible for	Self systemic
In a quandary	Power trip
Shat on my head!	Wire net
Lengthwise in the soup, and peel	These problems canteened, as you say
Over the car	Breaks are for
Nice fit she winked	*Love*
Back at the	Ranch
A restaurant	Song collided with the protestors' own
Shivers	Museum piece, a .44 calibre
Investments!	*Crawl*

Bargained for

Tulips

Surprise

Mother

Elastic

Rocket

Road

Achievements

Jungle

Jive

Peppercorns

Athabascan

Road Runner

Hamster

Fit

Tedlock

Frills

Furniture

Suit

Space

Buds

The weary black

Hole

Announced in light of

Dust on

Alberti's veil

Returns as

Positive power

Regime

Exudes

The Peppercorns

Next to Open Veins of Latin America

Paratactic

Brand name

Heroism

It if pleases

Bargained for   The economy

In the basement   In charge, Lamprey god

Alleluia!   Speaks

A reptile   Reptile

Skis

The saw   Oven

Elevator   Opening

Angle   The record

Adjudicates   Slide

Watermelon   In

Woke up   Illegally

Drove a nail into the head Stone

Dovetail   Peace

Marmaduke   Papers

Speak Spanish!   Parent

Luftwaffe   Divorced

Singles   From their past

Trumpets	Salute the flag
Enzymes	Tracers
Accordion	Of the fittest, said Clarke, who competed against 600 students from across
Lips	Their own swimming pool
Expostulating, exposing	Pregnancy
Gone for real, gonorrhea	Tests
Habits	Improve
Articles	Articling 'said Clarke'
Centipedes	For 80% who don't read
Uniform	Factory works
U-mate zoo	Concentration
Treats	*Matters* it
Topple	Surprise!
Toes	Dead length
Tight fit torque lift	To add
Cyclical	Weight
Bait	Sponge
Bores	Down

Strings attached   Hole

Tummy, then turns   Thing
    me this way

More!   Co-operates

Life!   Sigh

Lift!   Sign

Loft!   Dinosaurs surrender

                                Number

Number!

0

Cornius Flakius,

Theory-death of the snide, of the snide. SQUAWK!

Your questions catch me athwart
any new sense I might have of a
'poetics'

Oven Guard History
per mitts.
Protecting from immediacy,
        coffin stains.
Foot in the syrup – not good.

We have reached the permitted land
of Catatonia.

            – The Telepathic Parrot.

        duh cridic surferd frod
        a tradic medal iplojiod
        frohid podture oduh idood

Revlon, Teflon, Exxon: Easy-Off

                … a non-literary sense, certainly.

        Protagonists

            ' … expected so long
            they finally despaired
            of my coming.'

        They
        mean,
        sounds

captive
as –
before –

they're
made
mortal

trade
sends
them

They
work

goes
one

way
they

live
other.

North
per night.

Of course
They cost
The course
Of the
Course of

Courses of
Courses coursing
Off course
Coarse courses
Curses of

I believe in Truth! (Warheit)

'They carve
   in our own language
      yet I don't *recognize* them,

      because their *instruments* ... '

jab

          re-mind –
re-member   awaken – to
body to   bodily conditionals
'here'   das Ding – Ja! – mach ring
          job

'If the shoe kicks'

5.5 X 8.5

from the line of force as piped in
         I

     By Want Waters, Font
     Typed
     Face.

as well as from piping
Unlive dead end –
   undo typing?

'Go'

ahead, excuse me …

scared

to here   to

go 'hair'.

you are. if I hammer shortly.

That's far.

Homer, and hasn't changed much since

'I was headed, from the flashing end of a hammer, for the nail.'

Fluke shop

'If a word lies

speechless

Paint its tongue

Hang on wall.'

Nails
unfettered from their downy guilts.

'In fact, it could have been the nail *in* the head
as they couldn't speak our tongue
and begged, *pass the solution* … '

The solvent, mum.

Dampness, gloom, pockmarks walking
over the faces of the daughters …

'It's *that pimple*.'
ding and zing or something

Just grasping at social referents.
Das ding-a-ling. Seuss it out.

The marmoreal truth
terrified hatless
exercised with caution
on its hill.
Allegory – withered in its packing crate.

Return to bender.

'bent' as born

We regret to shoehorn you
with Bellini chisel.

Trait of the Union Dress

'Spunknik'

Credit card count-up
for a free launch

You first, spunknik.

-

the cosmos captive and deadly

Armageddon no answer

The asteroid
split like a fart

saving earth's
dinosaur

'America'
who will bite your ass ...

Frail barber says ...

Put this down
to playing
in your ears
with the air.

Among the buns, bun it.

Psycho Anal Eyes
                    says the lovely old song – rejects it
            'Good
            open mooning
            season,
            reverend!'

Church of Satan!

Just gasping for social efferents.
'Snaked his cake.'

        Pun is Rime

Of Homer's entrail

America is a forgotten art
        Flat, mediatized, power-friendly statement
tred in a lot
and crafts store in the German district

'It's really unfair.'
of a burnt star.

M. Manson votes G.W. Bush.
that built in is the connection, in each of us, to Cosmos

                                        Rock, rock, old Joe Clark.
                                        Rock, rock, I say.

        '*Rock* star ... Never thought of it before, like that.'

        'No twinkle, just – clock.' Diction, live thy pun.

                                'Emoluments' – payment
                                        for *corn-grinding* (OK?)

                        FLAKED MILLED CORN etc.
                        Proudly made in / ...
                        London, Ontario

Once snorting on its way

scene;   turn machine off, go to feeder

event;   think of Homer and pull

climax;   what comes; watch
                fingertips eyes, now.

crisis;   That's not even money.

hero;   It's a moneyed poem, they say

development;   that's what language looks like.

posture;
Explained, After Complete & Satisfactory Digestion, In One Easy Step
all that *meant*
The preferment, please.

      Pay us
      Takes us
      USA

      I HATE LOWER CASE

                  i'm the

                  sink of being
                  the drain of self in
                  pipes of plenty, and out.
                  – who am i?

                  Standard Average European (SAE).
                  Self-addressed envelope.

                  'Beer', mass noun.

RECEIPT! Am tryin' to say, *receipt* …

          Puts a swivel
          in your air, hair, chair.
          Squawks, no squeak.

Trickle-down

That's the way the urine's tinkled; goodnight.

From the rooftops
one crowbar drops
a BMW.

Konk!nomics

American style donut
job – no holes barred.

No punched through the air
looms.

Through the crap

They maked hours
come out of dung.

The ow act is coming back
for what
it never lacked.

'Do' donut.
'Not' nothin'.
'Do Not Grasp It'
'That's right, read the signs.'

'Doesn't mean much
in my money anyway.'
– How parrotic.

It's come, this
haunts.

So payfull.

out of appetite. Let this swirl –
('Feel a cartoon coming on.'
The stick emitted carrots.

'Here's stickin' it to ya!'
'If I can bring it up, I will.'

Smaller-font text – from Charles
Olson's 'Letter to Elaine Feinstein';
'Rock, rock, old Joe Clark … '
African-American folksong;

WELCOME TO THE GAS AGE

Reap week wall it
repays play dough
om doom Eeyore
out. Analysis no longer required

tearfully
displayed political
conviction from me
dia, specular agency

in inter
national markets defends capital
interest, let alone interest
in this with

out spelling it
out of
the game. The vet
bets the pet. Finch

hitters are quitters. Liars (tiniest nominalist
flinch)
walk? Coin
crumbles like the rest of it

spilling out, but for a hound dog's
mouth. Convinced
'if I cash my head
above the change

while I'm still far away
I'm in range'. Next exit
text haven. 'Agents of change sign on
anyone.' Anything? Zephyrs

to their lairs requesting
crosshatching for heritage status
blow job. Grease oozing back
as truth in accounting

firms' pipes. Expressions
of thatchwork counterculture.
'Your ducts and grease –
hicksville to me!'

'Feeling exposed gives me narrative
balls-massage.' 'I'm a
PG retiree.' 'Free
Feed Feelings.'

But don't counter your thatchwork before it's well laid,
or go gormless into the rooter, the motor,
the router, the scooter –
metaphor

matching socks. Take a wheezer.
Multiply by national parks.
Add a buyout.
Then offer noun asylum.

As a great leavener of human sediment
the party's 'can do' reactor
opens all fudged lines
tie-dying universals.

The soreshit enterprise life
still forms from Greimas's grid.
A grey mass puckers open
'and no plugs allowed … '

Swab the grease.
Iffy cultural swabs
a place with taste
in Kahlúa with the law.

Lawyer yayas out
side. Flaps
jack looks up 'bigfry'
in ideological dermis

— as charged. Massive
waste sitter
hangs the atom out:
hung-up in shingles.

'Nothing's left
inside except insides
of the outside, which are paid
for which you have to pay.'

Explains basement paranoia
about windows
and sign on door: 'Stranger
lives here'. Lone

loan
lake lot
prop. – your prime
ticket charge's skid

mark on the ass
vault and 'gimme' a sign,
shopworn
form extruded from

executive fineprint
in the haystack of freedom
to burp a camel.
The pompopus

came perilously close
to the ex
-it -ting
-uish or -tinc

-tion sign in the
lobby of love
where monitors roam
at the counting table

of Pembroke's arcade.
'Goes for broke
just keeps on
licking' the papers. Canadian

de Sadeians
for the Pollution of Onlookers
invite you to their annual Gunny Breather.
Paralysis no longer required

series of substitutions
on backs of tried phrases
goes this far appraising
'public' language after 'private'

structures social gaps.
'Gunny Quilture Sacks Fall Lineup.'
'Hemmed Still Ditches Uncertainty.'
'Quitter Currents Jam Picnic Hopes.'

What they say the
lips parade.
A fall for it.
Composition wreathes.

And Sean Connery

And Sean Connery – a favourite that rings up an impressive 221% ROI
rain or shine. This is merely the beginning,
saving in style
a world of culture and refinement

among people of taste and breeding,
your dog certainly has a surprised look on its face.
Oh that's because you're looking at his butt.
Then he's certainly not going to enjoy that uh treat I just gave him.

A man of passion will be framed
by a one-armed, -legged, -eyed
man, the year's most 'disarming'
comedy, America's most wanted

man, direct from a two thousand sixty two screen national release
and master of disguise.
I see you. And, I see you.
Backed with a fifty-day pay-per-view holdback.

I'm not going back. The man who commits
comedy, to the tune of an average 85% ROI.
I'm not wearing underwear.
It's not just a movie. It's every movie.

Now coming to the stage one of the all-time greats,
put your hands together, ladies and gentlemen.
Three different women.
Let me take care of this.

What kind of dog is that? Summer Doll? Some of this,
some of that? With one husband in common,
where's *my* husband? Direct from
a one thousand three hundred seventy-seven screen national release

with fifty-day pay-per-view holdback
and a sensational thirty-plus title star-studded original-hit soundtrack.
God, I'd give my right arm for a siren right now.
Get out of the way!

Yeah, that's him. Get me right up behind this
trailer. Watch your step. Look
both ways. And buckle up. But when all else fails, get lethal.
The gang's all here, ready to rack up rockin' ROI

in the redhot one hundred thirty million dollar box office
smash. Monroe didn't want to tell you this. My rope is breaking.
     You're gonna be a father.
Pile up the rental perks with this critically acclaimed HBO home
     video release.
They were legends on stage and screen. How'd all these people get
     into my room?

Working together and playing together – what's wrong with that?
You said action. We did the scene. You said cut. That's it.
Living large on fame, friendship and power, life was a game, and
     they were winning.
Twenty-four. A winner. My table. New rules, doll.

So they raised the stakes. Help me put your brother-in-law
in the White House. It was their
world. We lived in it. Irresistible
POP. Extended cross-trailering. Pay-per-view holdbacks.

1

A remumblery

Features drain from quotient
self.

Vague.
What's this?

It, speak.
I

dried.
Bullshit was *never* this

sweet. To write as if
I can

memory.
Defining human being

consumer for
generations.

Let it
have choice. Never think about where I am

from, although often
about myself!

'My name is Leif, and I, too,
am an accordion player.'

Effects ate the data, sorry.
What is the question?

To read Kafka as
if Gogol lived unemployed in Montréal

in the era of late Reagan
ate Mulroney.

Remember what?
Grief, hail, if

history is important, I'm not important, you are, and whatever else is out
here, just.

All loyalty to the social.
What a piece of shit. Scintillating!

Maxims from my best friend drinking.
The desiccation of American finance!

Can't
invoke

single perception. *Therefore 'perception'*
is out of touch. It's an abstraction, and he sells it.

Deaf bubble word live
in air porn.

They've got ability and the corporate database to access 'private parties'.
NB: No Party is under any obligation to *maintain* your Comments (and the

use of your name with any comments) in
confidence, to *pay* to you any compensation for any Comments

submitted, or to *respond* to any of your Comments.
Even though it's on, maybe you're not. Get it?

It's like *banning* the air.
You're under no obligation to comment.

You're over yes, and out. No
comment – throwing your work in the *private* face?

Content disarmed.
Complete this form and attach to your poem.

Poem? I may have gotten an optical illusion.
I've got personal alarms, for believing when I hear it – appointments,
    parking, dinner.

'Calling all'
and that curiouser and curiouser

'interpellating
one'

or 'a'
federal bureau of bugles at the

annunciation –
AOL, worth 12x more than it can possibly earn, buys Time Warner,
    who buys EMI.

Treating us like
or to, barkers. Join the right

signal.
Golf on

radio.
(Putt

meaning to
gather

again … Ball!)
Sordello

in Waco.
Militia muesli

mix, 3M.
'You can take this life and scud it.'

Why so many Chinese restaurants in Los Alamos?
For spying, of course. Find out what radio

stations Christians listen to in their cars.
DJ turntables have outsold guitars.

You're working with a wave-form diagram of iambic pentameter
adding delay and feedback

cutting out unwanted frequencies
applying phase effects

even buffing the sine waves.
World's oldest sound recordings

circa 1885, birth of Ezra Pound.
Help me communicate with human beings.

Social engineer wannabe, with
or without cognitive map

job? Bank of Montreal ad campaign
effect.

Verse
in the era of late petroleum ice cream.

Hospitalized for birth of explanation
I insist within the aesthetic village, as cornered as the next guide.

So much given, etc., in return, *revolution*
of personnel doors at best, you screen

for career.
Taste

tests – *What* a piece of bunk?
What *a* piece of bunk?

Whoever, or whatever, did the social inscriptions, italicized 'me',
  in the last analysis, first
of all, *and in a first* analysis.

We all screen
for I screens this

body over.
I am not a muse.

Here
alone but for interpellation

thanks to interpellation
disarm your tone. The father

you seem, the closure
I got, creamer's

aftertaste. I need billing bad.
O for a Be-in.

Pun's arbitrary need
history's.

Who's next!
Information Please.

Effects ate chance
operations *put body back*

together again. People of the non-, or internally
recirculating libido:

Here is the immanent utopia!
Answer answers with answers?

Go fuck yourself, therefore I am.
Every line, entitlement?

'Keeping it simple' *so that* 'we can observe ourselves'. What
historical logic! Don't *know* what

to do *and* don't know how to
do it. Do

fuss. Object in mind,
subject in relations.

Nobody move! Including
me. Face backwards in the text

as if out of this word
and pack as if for the last time.

Writing, to be wary of
otherwise effortless everyday un-

conscious production.
'The unconscious' is to 'no such entity' as

'I go inside the envelope others have written to me' is to
'I hate metaphors, similes, memories, time'.

The self-esteem evaporator is turned on now
TO OPEN THE BLANK ENVELOPE!

No one to address but one's own prospects
of death.

Nip 'n' tuck journalism just loves the wrinkles in Olay sales.
– NO GEEZERS FOR OIL –

Is it paving, or raving inside
or out? Need more quarters.

Someone is dying inside (abasement
dweller) vs someone who is dying

outside – 'I don't *have* a roof'. And the floor
is yours, authoritarian neoliberal

backed by police tactics. You're *welcome*.
Self-refining as you go, La Rochefoucault.

What a *piece* of shit.
'Watch where you walk.' Typical!

What's demeaning
The Meaning of Meaning?

So much Calvinism
so little charisma – philosophy

of insertion, getting a lock on key
themes. I'd hate to write *being*

or its philosophy.
Children's token happy-enterprise stories.

'The economy must expand.'
Connectors, for connections, dangling, live.

Wired for Arnold.
'Children are just like refrigerators'

economics an allegory of self-interest.
Describe what the reader will already know

and recognize when your craft is successful.
Luggage drops onto shifting, rotating black rubber strips –

oblong carousel. Not bad! Now describe
in this context, 'carousel'.

The one that enters those heavy-metal symbols of oldline industry.
They made sausage meat out of her pet pig.

International business machines are happy
to stand Grassroots United Against Reform's Demise

forever 'Stockwell Day' in Reform's country
or county.

Citizens of global activism, effects want to eat your data.
We farmed dispute settlement mechanisms, everybody's eating the results.

Midwest grain factories work their margin
far from places most people visit

to enjoy nature. Prince
Charles, talking to his plants

thinks with the bone in his nose.
Think horde. Pass the butler.

'Local' as placemat
at table with share, for egg, holder.

Animated like a Greek god
creates story – what is it?

All the young Murdochs, filling their baskets
when every egg counted.

Make wealth grow your own hair for you –
stock investment as hair loss treatment

conditioners (redundancy), for conditions, of possibility.
Clinton's face morphs into marble butt.

So peeled, so oxidized, so
long, apprenticeship

I'm my own banana now!
Workers wage

pressure
on darkness visible.

The oxymoron stared vacantly at its mission.
Monumentalism

reduced to dextrose tablet
in hike up mountain.

Haiku balancing
gauge itself. 'My job, to explain the beauties

of free markets.' My nipples
to stand in solidarity with Steelworkers

and Teamsters, and all the labouring people.
Explain 'nipples'.

I'm paramount in this theatre.
Paranormal, to you?

You can call me Horsey!
I'm glad to have issues for breasts.

Am I procrastinating the world, of, on, others' terms,
begging the question?

O fickle poelitics. I write the words
affecting *meow*?

Barbarism!
You taught much.

Now, you're dust.
Shame on us.

Made the whole
world singed.

Animal control
Strangers in the dark – emerging markets.

Companies … who need companies.
Japanese counterparts, our competitors

our friends; consumers, the enemy.
Ford trucks in supply lines of the Wehrmacht.

Intel corp's $327M gain from sales of investment shares boosted its
    net income to $2.4B
beating Wall Street estimates

for the quarter. Intel shares jumped about 13% last Friday on that
earnings report. Tao of management

Dow of faith. Time on my hands
never leaves a mark, as the person sleeping with

the person is the one
having the relationship – it's

win-win for the person.
Slap. Popularity skill's derrière-garde

is not wiped yet.
Kiss the marble butt

hello.
The blah blah blah of theory-weary theoretical bodies drinking coffee

agreed. Quoting
may indeed ritualize the banal, nevertheless, they –

advanced patheticism.
Our movement is indeed, catching

on something – 'Sorry!'
Stud me up, I'll never start.

Quit with the ghost roast – I *hate* that.
We don't need no mole control ... Hegel!

Being is for diamonds
and syllogisms.

Now, you're us.
Shame on dust.

What's the matter now?
Reading is un-believing.

You don't have to *read* Japanese
to *eat* Japanese

data.
I am a mental no

(saying) body.
I, ego?

Sure feel we tissue dissolving
conditionally – wet issue.

Mote of determination to every self
present sovereign, historical

precedent. Practice makes
me want

to pee.
What a –

his signature
is all over the placemat.

Complicit with the wristwatch.
Asshole.

Utopic? You toke it.
I must escort you to the door please.

Arresting party of four?
This way.

There would be goods to be good about.
NyQuil. *You* pick it.

I project

I feel source-fed this way
you get something

I'm afraid to say
some thing

saying
something they

put on me I
project

yet 'silvering' words
mirror limits

I fill and complete
the sentence where

there places
to go

speeds to clock
Marmaduke here

because I
love these

breeds phrases 'unknown
familiars' fed by

what
that

is
what (this is)

does that
what mean

meanderer want that
brackets demands

excoriates speech
'is that a body'

I small and humble
O load, untie these lands

'steel
syntax of

exploitation' I functions to state
a state where

I can meet up with it the country
in country of

of
barking

I will come back to this point of
a project for society

shortly I want something
left for you to describe

it
that

we share like this
itch I

don't want to work slogan
of travel industry

Ontario strikes for
them

something loose
enough provides

information
for what

this is
to

be about something
dimples to

kiss you substitute
for it

falls into
the arbitrary

penultimate gulf
starts making

'sense' starts NAFTA
kill ya Mexico

is in the news
or is the news

in Mexico 'I have an expression
to feed

relax and
build up

conjuncturally
opportunities

from structural
constraints

of profit
more to write of

always
from defeat

the feet on a ground
swell ink

Alan Davies Project

Water proof

How about that, voice.
How about that voice.
How about that choice.

How about that bit.
How about that, hoarse.
How about that drink forgets it.

How about that quartz awhile replaced it.
How about that quart.
How about that habit dressed to spill now.

For instance how about that backyard time.
And that body too eh.
How about that comma rhyme.

So long as it was way off, we could imagine
          it to be anything
     we liked.

The mannerist mock

wound the clock
          too fast for its
     mechanism.

Time tried, then died.
          No one was left
     to escape.

'I'm just having a timed time'

I had bread; I lost bread.
I made bread. Bread was my way.
Bread was too successful for me even.
Bread corrupted 'us cooks'. We ate batter raw,
wore it on our heads. Were we too cookie?
'Bread' wasn't an expression yet, it was
a way – now gone, alas,
the way of the salt wave. To
'be in the bread' was to have nice crust
and a fresh way with soft things
inside. Moist loaves, those days, slept fast, rose slow.
Nothing could threaten us – not the cliché of onions, whose smell
we'd need to soak up like it was our real job … That's all
threats I'll mention for now – don't
get me going; I'll cry! There was *never* a show
stopper moment, *each moment*
the showstopper. Yeast never let us
down – nor up without
a laugh (*when, if* we wanted yeast!).
I am less than the unwanted,
without bread now – a cadaverous abracadabra
of diminishing expectations.
I'm already diminished – no more
plot than 'slice in corner, wasted'.
I'm so wasted.

' – Here's me in a phonetic spike!'

Deep and continual
even in the circuitry – and all I got was
this lousy time lapse.

No relation to any time *I'd* recognize.
No means to relate it to any time I wouldn't recognize.
That's me.

Routine lap on motherboard
with naturally electric finesse, no shocks, shorts,
breakers, crashes. Just a little atmospheric static

effect – 'synthesis' caused by devices like you,
material like me.
It was the disappointment of products, it was the efficiency of the times.

Sapswirls

There's no far like so far.
So far, no good.
No hair care nor hood
and no groaning home.

.

There's a time then boom – fainting
on the tomb. Too much
mach for one to
tack; or make that lack.

.

Status: action.
Sad as a ration.
Satis
factional.

.

I was a botched Big Mac!
They delivered me raw,
my felt pen tipped
with cold saws.

.

The 'no' that I'm not
I'd rather – to dinner, thinner
O, to be finer.
'This is your timer.'

．

And this, your egg.
Go forth.
Screw you.
More brew.

．

Let dear ears be near ears
be choosy. Chew on Lucy
if she's juicy. – 'Scuse me?
Let heads be heads (if they love in bed).

．

If there wasn't, there should be.
If there couldn't – then, have mercy.
I'm moody, lead liners
must take me.

．

The dead lift the dead
into their heads. Careful, another
mood swings a head. Mellow rumoured
to be left well fed.

．

The mind argues lotions.
What about beer? *It's* soft.
Body's wearing mind.
Call it weather, wearing body.

.

How come I never feel relaxed?
What luxury
that here, you think what
am *I* doing? is this relaxing?

.

Qua train
car – you Empty! I'm hitching through on you.
These aren't hobo days, nor this
Mexico City Blues.

.

I respect you formally
attention's span 'here and now'
suffices, reminder old
habits out-sync'd with lip.

Coin Opera

Seek slim chance's margin
to write toward the don't-know still

repeal logic of punning difference
will coincide *on* words still

shame to leap no more and only speak
in the renaissance market still

going 'home' to the I am conserving this
body as good as a coffin still

driven from such givens
minces with them still

drafted to laughter a generation's ills
formed in a shell – with shells

to pay still one elephant down
the tubes at Hoover U is

the big to-do still
can't Harvard carpet how come

no hat for the Cat translates
favourite rhyme still

translated unwritten
memories brings oblique references

this side of the lyric still
I'd have hoped differently if

there was something else to ask for still
time to read about appalling hurt

finds, alert, this, still.

The ethical distributor

was plugged in or

kicked in.

0

138

Cornius Flakius,
The ethical distributor:
Poetry is information
A remumblery
I project.

Grease Earn,
The Good Beaver (1996):
I'm just having a timed time
Clone jacking
Alan Davies Project
And Sean Connery.

Grind on
Guatemala
Truth build up
Disposed
The Mood Embosser:
WELCOME TO THE GAS AGE.

Curdles:
– Here's me in a phonetic spike!
The importants of being
The mannerist mock
Coin opera?
Perma
Sapswirls

Posy:
Fey lure
So how's the Dow
Yield
Slung low – *sell high*

Water proof:
Social logic
Unconscious needs
Accident accumulates intent.

Acknowledgements

Thanks to editors David Bromige and Jack Kimball (*The East Village*, www.theeastvillage.com), Stephen Cain, Suzanne Zelazo and Natalee Caple (*Queen Street Quarterly*), Emily Cargan and Fred Wah (*dANDelion*), Kyle Conner and Greg Fuchs (*Highwire Yearbook*), Jeff Derksen, Peter Jaeger and Scott Pound (*Open Letter*), the *filling Station* collective circa 1999, Bob Harrison and Andrew Levy (*Crayon*), Michael Magee (*Combo*), Rob Manery (*hole*), Kathryn McLeod and Douglas Stetar (*Motel*), Chris and Jenn McCreary (*ixnay*), Laura Moriarty (*non* <socrates.berkeley.edu/~moriarty>), and Aaron Vidaver and Robyn Laba and the *W* collective circa 2000, who all published some of these poems. Thanks also to Dennis Barone and Peter Ganick for 'Grease Earn' in *The Art of Practice: 45 Contemporary Poets* (Elmwood, CT: Potes & Poets Press, 1994); to derek beaulieu for *Curdles*, a chapbook (Calgary: housepress, 2001) and 'Yield' in Voices: *Poems for Karl and Talon* (Calgary: housepress, 2001); and to Miles Champion and Sheila Lawson, for 'Manifester' in *Resolute* (London, England: Platform Gallery, 2000). Special thanks to Jeff Derksen, Nicole Markotić, damian lopes, Darren Wershler-Henry and Alana Wilcox. Each of you has made indispensible suggestions for the text in its present form. I'd like to especially thank Darren, who made this book possible. Thanks also to Dale McFarland at Frith Street Gallery, London, England, and to Cornelia Parker, for a photo of one of her installations, 'Matter and What It Means' (the installation consists of coins that have been run over by a train, suspended over a shadow made of dirty money. 1989. Photographed by Edward Woodman).

Typeset in Minion
at the Coach House on bpNichol Lane, 2002

Copy edited and proofread by Alana Wilcox
Designed by damian lopes
Cover design by Darren Wershler-Henry
Cover art by Cornelia Parker

To read the online version of this text and other titles from
Coach House Books, visit our website:
www.chbooks.com

To add your name to our e-mailing list, write:
mail@chbooks.com

Toll-free:
1 800 367 6360

Coach House Books
401 Huron Street on bpNichol Lane
Toronto, Ontario
M5S 2G5